of Lisieux

Compiled and introduced by
Don Mullan

First published in 2002 by

the columba press

55A Spruce Avenue, Stillorgan Industrial Park,
Blackrock, Co Dublin

Designed by Bill Bolger
Cover photograph © Office Central de Lisieux
Origination by The Columba Press
Printed in Ireland by
ColourBooks Ltd, Dublin

ISBN 1 85607 373 4

To
Fr J. Linus Ryan O Carm
and
Sr Mary Brigeen ODC

and the Discalced Carmelite Nuns,
Loretto, Pennsylvania

friends of Thérèse I respect and value

Acknowledgements

The publisher and editor gratefully acknowledge the permission of the following to quote from material in their copyright: Darton, Longman & Todd Ltd for quotations from *Maurice and Thérèse* by Patrick Ahern; Continuum for quotations from *Collected Letters of St Thérèse of Lisieux*, translated by F. J. Sheed; Fontana Religious for quotations from *Story of a Soul*, translated by Ronald Knox; ICS Publications for quotations from *Story of a Soul* and *St Thérèse of Lisieux - Her Last Conversations*, translated by John Clarke OCD, *The Poetry of Saint Thérèse of Lisieux*, translated by Donald Kinney OCD, and *The Prayers of St Thérèse of Lisieux*, translated by Aletheia Kane OCD.

Author's Acknowledgements

Sincere thanks are owed to the following for their kind support and assistance with this publication:

To my good friends, Mother John of the Cross and the Discalced Carmelite Nuns, Loretto, Pennsylvania; Fr J. Linus Ryan O Carm for his friendship and guidance; Bernie Bergin for her assistance with parallel reading and much goodwill, good humour and encouragement; Seamus Cashman; John Scally and Emer Ryan for their continued friendship; the following members of the Carmelite family for their varied and most helpful suggestions (my apologies in advance for not being able to incorporate all): Sr M. Brigeen; Sr M. Helen Thérèse; Sr Mary Eilish McKenna; Sr Mary Gabrielle; Sr Marie Thérèse; Sr Mary Noleen of Jesus; Anonymous; Sr M. Kevin; Sr M. Philomena; Sr M. Immaculata; Sr Brigid; Sr Mary Attracta Thérèse; Sr Anne; Sr Damian; Sr Mary Joseph Byrne; Sr Thérèse Marie of the Holy Face; Sr Anne; Sr Mary Brigid (Nigeria); Sr M. Philomena; Sr M. Thérèse Elizabeth; Sr Mary Magdelen Dineen; Sr Mary Catherina; Sr Marie of the Sacred Heart; Marie O'Grady; Oonagh Twomey; Margaret O'Neill; Fr Pat Beecher ODC; Fr Philip Brennan O Carm. Finally, to my family, Margaret, Thérèse, Carl and Emma for their continued kindness and support.

St Thérèse of Lisieux was born at Alençon, France, on 2 January 1873. Her parents, Louis Martin and Zèlie Guérin, were deeply religious. Thérèse referred to them as 'more worthy of heaven than of earth'.

In April 1888, aged 15, she entered the enclosed order of Carmelites in Lisieux.

Three of Thérèse's four sisters, Pauline, Marie and Céline, also joined the Lisieux Carmel. Her fourth sister, Léonie, joined the enclosed order of Visitation nuns in nearby Caen.

Thérèse died in 1897, aged 24. A year later, the publication of her autobiography, *Histoire d'une âme – Story of a Soul*, revealed to the world a hidden life of unconditional love of God and neighbour,

lived with heroic passion. Her motto was:
'Love is repaid by love alone,' which she
borrowed from her great religious mentor,
St John of the Cross.

Thérèse's constant companions were the
gospels in which she discovered the source
of the Trinity – *Merciful Love. Merciful
Love* became the burning obsession of her
life, the source of her vocation and the
prophetic boldness through which she saw

no discontinuity between life and death. The following quotations and prayers are the living words of a young saint who continues to inspire millions throughout the globe. Thérèse is Co-Patroness of the Missions and in 1997, the centenary of her death, she was named a Doctor of the Church.

Don Mullan.
Dublin
22 August 2002

DESIRE TO LOVE

… to love Jesus, to be his victim of love …
The desire alone to be a victim suffices,
but we must consent to remain
always poor and without strength,
and this is the difficulty,
for the truly poor in spirit:
where do you find him?

DESIRE TO LOVE

In order to live in one single act of perfect love, I offer myself as a victim of holocaust to your merciful love, asking you to consume me incessantly, allowing the waves of infinite tenderness shut up within you to overflow into my soul, and that thus I may become a martyr of your love, O my God!

LOVE

I understood that
love comprised all vocations,
that love was everything,
that it embraced all times and places …
in a word, that it was eternal!

LOVE

In the excess of my delirious joy,
I cried out: O Jesus, my love …
my vocation, at last I have found it …
my vocation is love!

LOVE

… without love all works are nothing,
even the most dazzling,
such as raising the dead to life
and converting peoples.

… in the heart of the church, my mother,
I shall be love.
Thus I shall be everything,
and thus my dream will be realised.

LOVE

… a soul that is burning with love
cannot remain inactive.

To love is to give everything.
It's to give oneself.

GOD

For God
the whole universe is just one speck.

GOD

How can I fear the one whom I love?

GOD'S LOVE

The sun's light,
that plays on the cedar-trees,
plays on each tiny flower
as if it were the only one in existence;
and in the same way
our Lord takes a special interest
in each soul,
as if there were no other like it.

GOD'S LOVE

The good God
has always treated me
like a spoiled child …
He has always made me desire
whatever he wanted to give me.

HOLY COMMUNION

I felt that I was loved …
it was no longer simply a look,
it was a fusion; they were no longer two,
Thérèse had vanished as a drop of water
is lost in the immensity of the ocean.

GOD'S WILL

When the human heart
gives itself to God,
it loses nothing of its innate tenderness;
in fact, this tenderness grows
when it becomes more pure
and more divine.

GOD'S WILL

We have only the one day of this life …
to give Our Lord some proof of our love.
The tomorrow of this day
will be eternity …

GOD'S WILL

Jesus wants
to possess your heart completely.
He wants you to be a great saint.

The good God never asks the impossible.

God's Guidance

Jesus has no need of books
or teachers to instruct souls:
He teaches without the noise of words.

GOD'S GUIDANCE

I have only to cast a glance in the gospels
and immediately I breathe in
the perfumes of Jesus' life,
and I know on which side to run.
I don't hasten to the first place
but to the last.

GOD'S GUIDANCE

My little boat has much trouble
making harbour.
For a long time I have seen the shore,
but I keep on finding
that I'm further from it;
still Jesus is steering my little ship
and I am sure …
he will bring it happily to port.

SIN AND WEAKNESS

When we cast our faults
into the devouring fire of love
with total childlike trust,
how would they not be consumed
so that nothing is left of them?

SIN AND WEAKNESS

For those who love him,
and after each fault come to ask pardon …
Jesus trembles with joy.

SIN AND WEAKNESS

One could believe
that it is because I haven't sinned
that I have such great confidence in God.
Really, if I had committed
all possible crimes,
I would always have the same confidence.

MERCIFUL LOVE

God is nothing but mercy and love.

There is no one who could frighten me,
for I know too well what to believe
concerning his mercy and his love.

MERCIFUL LOVE

God's justice seems to me
clothed in love …
he takes into account our weakness,
he is perfectly aware
of our fragile nature.
What then should I fear?

MERCIFUL LOVE

If I were to die at the age of eighty,
if I were in China, anywhere,
I would still die, I feel,
as little as I am today.
And it is written: 'At the end,
the Lord will rise up to save the gentle
and the humble of the earth.'
It doesn't say 'to judge,' but 'to save'.

MERCIFUL LOVE

As far as little ones are concerned,
they will be judged with great gentleness.

MERCIFUL LOVE

Having prepared me
to appear before you ...
may my soul take its flight
without any delay
into the eternal embrace
of your merciful love ...

MERCIFUL LOVE

O my God,
I want to base my hope in you alone.
Since you can do everything,
deign to bring to birth in my soul
the virtue I desire.
To obtain this grace of your infinite
mercy I will very often repeat:
'O Jesus, gentle and humble of heart,
make my heart like yours!'

FORGIVENESS

… nobody is a good judge in his own case.

OBEDIENCE

What anxieties the vow of obedience
frees us from!
How happy are simple religious!

OBEDIENCE

I am a little brush
that Jesus has chosen
in order to paint his own image
in the souls entrusted to my care.

PERFECTION

Perfection consists simply
in doing his will,
and being just what he wants us to be.

PERFECTION

I realise now that
perfection means putting up with
other people's shortcomings,
feeling no surprise at their weaknesses,
finding encouragement
even in the slightest evidence
of good qualities in them.

PERFECTION

Since one can take my little acts of virtue
for imperfections,
one can also be mistaken
in taking for virtue
what is nothing but imperfection.

GRACE

Everything is a grace!

The soul, when in a state of grace,
has nothing to fear from the spirits of evil;
they are cowards,
so cowardly that they run away
at a glance from a child.

GRACE

I find, just when I need them,
certain lights that I had not seen until
then, and it isn't most frequently during
my hours of prayers that these are
abundant but rather in the midst of
my daily occupations.

GRACE

Set free from the world
And without any support,
Your grace overwhelms me,
My only friend!

TROUBLES AND SUFFERING

It is most consoling to remember
that Jesus, the Strong God,
experienced our weakness,
that he trembled at the sight
of his own bitter chalice,
the very one which he had once
so ardently desired to drink.

TROUBLES AND SUFFERING

I'm suffering very much,
but am I suffering very well?
That's the point!

TROUBLES AND SUFFERING

Above the clouds
the sky is always blue.

TROUBLES AND SUFFERING

It is surely true that a drop of gall
must be mingled in every cup,
but I find that trials help us
to detach ourselves from the earth;
they make us look higher than this world.

HAPPINESS AND JOY

I always find a way
to be happy
and to profit from my miseries.

HAPPINESS AND JOY

True happiness cannot be found here …
My only peace, my only happiness,
My only love is you, Lord!

CHARITY

The point which came home to me most
of all was that it was no good leaving
charity locked up in the depths of your
heart. The cheerful light of charity isn't
meant simply for the people we are fond
of; it is meant for everybody in the house,
without exception.

CHARITY

Charity must not consist in feelings
but in works.

It is only charity
that can expand my heart.

CHARITY

When charity has buried its roots
deeply within the soul,
it shows itself externally.

GOOD WORKS

Anything which is good in me
is the effect of God's mercy
– that and nothing else.

GOOD WORKS

The only true glory, I soon realised,
is the glory that lasts for ever;
and, to want that, you don't need
to perform any dazzling exploits
– you want to live a hidden life,
doing good in such an unobtrusive way …

GOOD WORKS

The most beautiful thoughts
are nothing
without good works.

DOUBT

God permitted my soul to be invaded by
the thickest darkness, and the thought of
heaven, up until then so sweet to me,
[became] the cause of struggle and
torment. This trial was to last not a few
days or a few weeks, it was not to be
extinguished until the hour set
by God himself ...

Doubt

It is true that at times a very small ray
of the sun comes to illumine my darkness,
and then the trial ceases for an instant,
but afterward the memory of this ray,
instead of causing me joy,
makes my darkness even more dense.

DOUBT

There are souls
for whom God's mercy
never tires of waiting
and to whom he grants his light
only by degrees.

FAITH

What a grace it is to have faith!
If I had no faith,
I would have inflicted death on myself
without hesitating a moment!

FAITH

We who run in the way of love
shouldn't be thinking of sufferings
that can take place in the future;
it's a lack of confidence,
it's like meddling in the work of creation.

FAITH

No, nothing worries me.
Nothing can trouble me.
My soul knows how to fly
 higher than the lark.

SIMPLICITY

True greatness is to be found in the soul,
not in a name.

SIMPLICITY

I want sweetness and purity
To shine on your brow,
But the virtue that I give you
Above all is simplicity.

SIMPLICITY

The closer one approaches God,
the simpler one becomes.

SIMPLICITY

I love only simplicity;
I have a horror for 'pretence'.

PRIDE

Compliments are at their best
when you aren't meant to hear them;
and the thrill of pleasure I felt
made me realise that I was full of pride.

PRIDE

… vanity slips so easily into the heart.

HUMILITY

The whole point of love
is making yourself small.

HUMILITY

To enjoy these riches
we must be humbled
and recognise our nothingness,
and that is what so many
are not willing to do.

HUMILITY

It is to God alone
that all value must be attributed;
there's nothing of value
in my little nothingness.

MATERIAL WEALTH

… joy isn't found
in the material objects surrounding us
but in the inner recesses of the soul.

Material wealth

We have seen beautiful things in Paris,
but all this is not happiness …
the beauties of Paris
do not win my heart in the least.

MATERIAL WEALTH

On earth we must be attached to nothing,
not even to the most innocent things,
for they fail you
just when you least expect it.
Only the things that are eternal
can content us.

POVERTY

I have nothing but God, alone, alone.

I do not feel the pinch of poverty
since I never lack anything.

POVERTY

I have renounced the goods of this earth
through the vow of poverty,
and so I haven't the right to complain
when one takes a thing that is not mine ...
I should rejoice when it happens
that I feel the pinch of poverty.

POVERTY

I hold nothing in my hands.
Everything I have, everything I merit
is for the church and for souls.
If I were to live to eighty,
I will always be as poor as I am now.

PEACE

In the bottom of my heart
I felt a great peace,
since I had done everything in my power
to answer what God was asking of me.

PEACE

Why speak of a delirious joy?
No, this expression is not exact,
for it was rather the calm and serene peace
of the navigator perceiving the beacon
which must lead him to the port …

Peace

I am very far from practising
what I understand,
and still the desire alone I have of doing it
gives me peace.

TRUTH

I cannot express in words
what happened in my soul;
what I know is that the Lord illumined it
with rays of truth
which so surpassed the dark brilliance
of earthly feasts
that I could not believe my happiness.

TRUTH

I never looked for anything
but the truth;
I have understood humility of heart.

TRUTH

There is no one who could frighten me,
for I know too well what to believe
concerning his mercy and his love.

SCHOOLDAYS

I have often heard it said
that the time spent at school
is the best and happiest of one's life.
It wasn't this way for me.
The five years I spent in school
were the saddest of my life.

SCHOOLDAYS

… my greatest successes were history and composition. All my teachers looked upon me as a very intelligent student, but it wasn't like that at uncle's house where I was taken for a little dunce, good and sweet, and with right judgment, yes, but incapable and clumsy.

Schooldays

They often spoke highly of the
intelligence of others in my presence,
but of mine they never said a word,
and so I concluded I didn't have any and
was resigned to see myself deprived of it.

PARENTS

The good God gave me
a father and mother
more worthy of heaven than of earth.

PARENTS

Children learn the secret of holiness
– that is, the song of divine love –
from those who are entrusted
with their education
just as birds learn to sing
by listening to the parent bird.

PARENTS

A mother's heart is more discerning
than a doctor's,
for it knows how to guess
at what is suitable for its child's sickness.

PARENTS

O you who knew
how to create the mother's heart,
I find in you
the tenderest of Fathers!

WOMEN

I still cannot understand why women
are so easily excommunicated in Italy,
for every minute someone was saying:
'Don't enter here! Don't enter there,
you will be excommunicated!'
Ah! poor women,
how they are misunderstood!

WOMEN

And yet women love God
in much larger numbers than men do,
and during the passion of Our Lord,
women had more courage than the apostles
since they braved the insults
of the soldiers
and dared to dry the adorable face of
Jesus.

PRIESTS AND RELIGIOUS

I lived for a month
among a lot of good holy priests,
and came to realise that
although their high office
makes them take rank above the angels,
they have their frailties
and their weaknesses like other men.

Your children will gather
the fragrance of flowers.
By doing this they wish to make amends
for all that priestly and religious souls
make you suffer by their offences.

In the smallest things
as well as the greatest,
God gives the hundredfold in this life
to those souls who leave everything
for love of him.

PRIESTS AND RELIGIOUS

I feel in me the vocation of the priest.
With what love, O Jesus, I would carry
you in my hands when, at my voice, you
would come down from heaven. And with
what love would I give you to souls! But
Alas! While desiring to be a priest, I
admire and envy the humility of St
Francis of Assisi and I feel the vocation of
imitating him in refusing the sublime
dignity of the priesthood.

Mother of sorrows and of love,
out of compassion for your beloved Son,
open in our hearts deep wells of love,
so that we may console him
and give him a generation of priests
formed in your school
and having all the tender thoughtfulness
of your own spotless love.

FRIENDS

How did Jesus love his disciples
and why did he love them?
Ah! It was not their natural qualities
that could have attracted him,
since there was between him and them
an infinite distance ...
still Jesus called them his friends,
his brothers.

FRIENDS

I understood how imperfect
was my love for my sisters.
I saw I didn't love them
as God loves them.

FRIENDS

When I wish to increase this love in me,
and when especially the devil tries
to place before the eyes of my soul
the faults of a sister
who is less attractive to me,
I hasten to search out her virtues,
her good intentions.

PRAYER

I just do what children have to do
before they've learnt to read –
I tell God what I want quite simply,
without any splendid turns of phrase,
and somehow he always manages
to understand me.

PRAYER

What would I do
without prayer and sacrifice?
They are all the strength I've got,
the irresistible weapons
our Lord has granted me.
I've proved it again and again
– they touch souls much more surely
than any words can.

PRAYER

There are certain things
that lose their perfume
as soon as they are exposed to the air;
there are deep spiritual thoughts which
cannot be expressed in human language
without losing their intimate
and heavenly meaning.

PRAYER

I should be desolate for dozing
during my hours of prayer
and my thanksgivings
after Holy Communion; well I am not.
I remember that little children
are as pleasing to their parents
when asleep as when they are wide awake.

PRAYER

For me, prayer is an aspiration of the
heart, it is a simple glance directed to
heaven, it is a cry of gratitude and love in
the midst of trial as well as joy; finally, it
is something great, supernatural, which
expands my soul and unites me to Jesus.

BLESSED VIRGIN MARY

If some disturbance overtakes me,
some embarrassment,
I turn very quickly to the Blessed Virgin
and as the most tender of mothers
she always takes care of my interests.

Blessed Virgin Mary

O Mary, if I were Queen of Heaven
and you were Thérèse,
I would want to be Thérèse
so that you might be Queen of Heaven!

BLESSED VIRGIN MARY

Oh! I love you, Mary,
saying you are the servant
of the God whom you charm
by your humility.
This hidden virtue
makes you all-powerful.
It attracts the Holy Trinity
into your heart.

BLESSED VIRGIN MARY

Later in Bethlehem, O Joseph and Mary!
I see you rejected by all the villagers.
No one wants to take in poor foreigners.
There's room for the great ones ....

Blessed Virgin Mary

There's room for the great ones,
and it's in a stable
the Queen of Heaven
must give birth to a God.
O my dearest Mother,
how lovable I find you,
how great I find you
in such a poor place!

TIME

Two thousand years
are not more in the Lord's eyes
than are twenty years,
than even a single day.

TIME

My life is but an instant, a passing hour.
My life is but a day
that escapes and flies away.
O my God!
You know that to love you on earth
I only have today.

TIME

Instead of wasting time
picking up little bits of straw,
one can dig for diamonds.

DEATH

Our happiest times on earth
must end in darkness.
It's only the first experience
of our final, eternal communion in heaven
that can be a day without sunset.

DEATH

I am not dying, I am entering into life.

What a surprise we shall have
at the end of the world
when we shall read the story of souls!

DEATH

Oh, certainly, I shall cry when I see God!
No, we can't cry in heaven.
Yes, we can, since it is said:
'And God will wipe away every tear
from their eyes.'

DEATH

I often repeated to myself a line of poetry
which brought peace and strength
back into my soul: it runs,
'Time's but a ship that bears thee,
not thy home.'

HEAVEN

In the eternal abode
of the King of heaven …
there will no longer be
the sadness of departings,
and it will be no longer necessary
to have some souvenir …
for his home will be ours for all eternity.

HEAVEN

I would like to run
through the fields of heaven ...
I would like to run in its fields
where the grass doesn't crumble,
where there are beautiful flowers
which don't fade, and beautiful children
who would be little angels.

HEAVEN

In heaven …
we shall see everything but sarcophaguses,
for there will be no tombs in heaven.

HEAVEN

I find, in moments of great grief,
one feels the need to look up to heaven;
there they are not weeping,
but all are joyful because Our Lord has
one more among his elect …
all are in the rapture of divine ecstasy,
they marvel that we can give the name of
death to the commencement of life.

CALL TO HOLINESS

I knew that I was loved,
and I, in my turn,
told God that I loved him,
and was giving myself to him
for all eternity.

I want always to be a little grain of sand
– I want to be a saint.

I offered myself to the Child Jesus as his
little plaything: I told him not to use me
as a valuable toy children are content to
look at but dare not touch, but to use me
like a little ball of no value which he could
throw on the ground, push with his foot,
pierce, leave in a corner,
or press to his heart if it pleased him.

CALL TO HOLINESS

I want to seek out a means
of going to heaven by a little way,
a way that is very straight, very short,
and totally new.

DOING GOOD UPON EARTH

If God answers my desires,
my heaven will be spent on earth
until the end of the world.
Yes, I want to spend my heaven
in doing good on earth.

DOING GOOD UPON EARTH

Everyone will see
that everything comes from God.
Any glory that I shall have
will be a gratuitous gift from God
and will not belong to me.
Everybody will see this clearly.